# The Big Green Poetry Machine

## Poems From The South
### Edited by Claire Tupholme

First published in Great Britain in 2008 by:
Young Writers
Remus House
Coltsfoot Drive
Peterborough
PE2 9JX
Telephone: 01733 890066
Website: www.youngwriters.co.uk

All Rights Reserved

© Copyright Contributors 2008

SB ISBN 978-1 84431 714 1

# Foreword

Young Writers' Big Green Poetry Machine is a showcase for our nation's most brilliant young poets to share their thoughts, hopes and fears for the planet they call home.

Young Writers was established in 1991 to nurture creativity in our children and young adults, to give them an interest in poetry and an outlet to express themselves. Seeing their work in print will encourage them to keep writing as they grow, and become our poets of tomorrow.

Selecting the poems has been challenging and immensely rewarding. The effort and imagination invested by these young writers makes their poems a pleasure to enjoy reading time and time again.

# Contents

**Brentwood Prep School, Brentwood**
| | |
|---|---:|
| Thomas Baker  (10) | 1 |
| Inigo Taylor  (10) | 2 |
| Edward Marling  (10) | 3 |
| Matthew Perry  (10) | 4 |
| Fleur Sumption  (10) | 5 |
| Lily Ball  (10) | 6 |
| Hannah Barnbrook  (9) | 7 |
| Kimia Khorshid  (9) | 8 |
| Ryan Norman  (10) | 9 |
| Sara Linney  (10) | 10 |

**Churcham Primary School, Churcham**
| | |
|---|---:|
| Ben Hazlewood  (8) | 11 |
| Katie Hyett  (8) | 12 |
| Joseph Lunnon  (11) | 13 |
| Warren Greaves  (8) | 14 |
| Oliver Snell  (8) | 15 |
| Emily Arkell  (9) | 16 |
| Harriet Price  (8) | 17 |
| Georgia Matthews  (9) | 18 |
| Ben Fisher  (9) | 19 |
| William Sekinger  (10) | 20 |
| Adam Rees  (11) | 21 |
| Alannah Hyett  (10) | 22 |

**Dame Bradbury's School, Saffron Walden**
| | |
|---|---:|
| Alexander Brett  (8) | 23 |
| Martin John Booyens  (8) | 24 |
| Katie Rushton  (9) | 25 |
| William Palmer  (9) | 26 |
| Francesca Simmons | 27 |
| Harriet Lander  (9) | 28 |
| Maddy Ball  (9) | 29 |
| Olivia Richardson  (9) | 30 |
| Euan Buchanan  (9) | 31 |
| Ella Horwell  (9) | 32 |
| Ben James  (8) | 33 |
| Oliver Snell  (9) | 34 |

| | |
|---|---|
| Ethan Monks  (9) | 35 |
| Lucy Clements  (9) | 36 |
| Louis Bartlett  (9) | 37 |
| Oliver Turpin  (9) | 38 |
| Andrew Williams  (9) | 39 |
| Plum Thatcher  (9) | 40 |
| Laura Cox  (9) | 41 |
| Cameron Lewis  (9) | 42 |
| Josie Taylor  (9) | 43 |
| Ryan Spencer  (9) | 44 |
| Sam Featherstone  (9) | 45 |
| Olivia Ross-Adams  (8) | 46 |

## Great Berry Primary School, Basildon

| | |
|---|---|
| Elizabeth Curno  (9) | 47 |
| Michael Burdett  (10) | 48 |
| Emma Jane Gadsdon  (10) | 49 |
| Âine Griffiths  (9) | 50 |
| Harry Browse  (10) | 51 |
| Chloe Harvey  (10) | 52 |
| Erin Mollie Rose Draper  (9) | 53 |
| Emily Morgan  (9) | 54 |
| Bayley Archer  (10) | 55 |
| Samuel Thomas  (9) | 56 |
| Kennedy Gorrie  (9) | 57 |
| Faye Schuster  (10) | 58 |
| Hannah Mathieson-Cheater  (10) | 59 |
| Megan Kendrick  (10) | 60 |
| Jennifer Munro  (10) | 61 |
| Lucia Freeman  (10) | 62 |
| Phoebe Peters  (9) | 63 |
| Toby Callaghan  (9) | 64 |
| Nicholas Like  (10) | 65 |
| Erica Wilks  (9) | 66 |
| Emily Lizzimore  (9) | 67 |
| Amy McMillan  (9) | 68 |
| Kwabena Adu-Poku  (10) | 69 |
| Claire Poulter  (9) | 70 |
| Tom England  (9) | 71 |
| Joseph Dulieu-Hasler  (10) | 72 |
| Jonathon Bartlett  (10) | 73 |

| | |
|---|---|
| Stacey O'Connor  (10) | 74 |
| Matthew Deaville  (10) | 75 |
| Samuel Baughan  (10) | 76 |
| Jon Andrews  (10) | 77 |
| Zeeshan Rasool  (10) | 78 |
| Michael Wright  (10) | 79 |
| Daanish Ahmad  (10) | 80 |
| Celine Vadher  (10) | 81 |
| Ross Pavelin  (10) | 82 |
| Georgia Chandler  (10) | 83 |
| Ryan Foss  (9) | 84 |
| Joe McKean  (10) | 85 |
| Courtney Treadwell | 86 |

**Limes Farm Junior School, Chigwell**

| | |
|---|---|
| Luke Cullen  (9) | 87 |
| Charlotte Tillbrook  (8) | 88 |
| Paris-Jade Clarke-Brown  (8) | 89 |
| Naseema Khalique  (11) | 90 |
| Naomi Alade  (8) | 91 |
| Ryan Snedker  (9) | 92 |

**Longcot & Fernham CE Primary School, Longcot**

| | |
|---|---|
| Christopher Morris  (8) | 93 |
| Holly Carlisle  (9) | 94 |
| Lucy Kent  (9) | 95 |
| Luke Parry  (8) | 96 |
| Josh Sheppard  (9) | 97 |
| Louise Jenkins  (8) | 98 |
| Natasha Hingston  (9) | 99 |
| Georgia Stevens  (11) | 100 |
| Albert George Durham  (10) | 101 |
| Jenny Fotheringham  (9) | 102 |
| Yasmin Dowell  (11) | 103 |
| Zoe Dowell  (11) | 104 |
| Joe Timms  (11) | 105 |
| William Casey  (10) | 106 |
| Jake Thacker-Pugsley  (9) | 107 |
| Kelsey-Louise Townsend  (11) | 108 |
| Jess Brader  (10) | 109 |
| Matthew Owens  (10) | 110 |

| | |
|---|---|
| Samuel Cooper  (10) | 111 |
| Adam Rich  (11) | 112 |
| Alice Keegan  (10) | 113 |
| Hannah Laura Jones  (10) | 114 |
| George Timms  (10) | 115 |
| Richard Cole  (11) | 116 |
| Natascha Blesing  (11) | 117 |
| Georgina Elbrow  (10) | 118 |
| Kayleigh Booth  (11) | 119 |
| William Peregrine  (10) | 120 |

**Mountnessing Primary School, Mountnessing**

| | |
|---|---|
| Oliver Bolton  (11) | 121 |
| Maisie Grover  (10) | 122 |
| Alex Horsnell  (10) | 123 |
| Harry Strickland  (11) | 124 |
| Aimee Parker  (10) | 125 |
| Bethanie Monk  (11) | 126 |

**St Peter's Catholic Primary School, Gloucester**

| | |
|---|---|
| Natalie Roy  (8) | 127 |
| Niamh Valentine  (9) | 128 |
| Katia D'Amato  (9) | 129 |
| Tristan Chong  (9) | 130 |
| Isaura Barr  (9) | 131 |
| Kieran Fox  (9) | 132 |
| Kimberley Travell  (9) | 133 |
| Kenneth De La Cruz  (9) | 134 |
| Zoe Limbrick  (9) | 135 |
| Mariya Rajesh  (8) | 136 |
| Jacob Foster  (8) | 137 |
| Alisha Perkins  (9) | 138 |
| Matthew Cantillion  (9) | 139 |
| Shaun Kent  (9) | 140 |
| Callum Jake McFarlane  (9) | 141 |
| Been Jude  (9) | 142 |
| Patrick Sharpe  (9) | 143 |
| Kyran Phillips  (9) | 144 |
| Elijah Jack Simpson  (9) | 145 |
| Leo Gregory Ashby  (9) | 146 |
| Allen Shaji  (9) | 147 |

| | |
|---|---|
| Shaun Elias (9) | 148 |
| Baylee Yani Myatt (9) | 149 |
| Sophie Harris (8) | 150 |
| Declan McGauley (8) | 151 |
| Willow Burden (9) | 152 |
| Marcus Taylor (9) | 153 |
| Amitha Susan Alex (9) | 154 |
| Joseph Hill (8) | 155 |
| Harley Brown Pollok (9) | 156 |
| Lauren McMahon (9) | 157 |
| Tara McGurk (9) | 158 |

**St Thomas More Catholic Primary School, Cheltenham**

| | |
|---|---|
| Alex Regan (8) | 159 |
| Josh Domm (8) | 160 |
| Leanne Maria Lusmore (8) | 161 |
| Zea Melania Cuciurean (8) | 162 |

**St Thomas More Catholic Primary School, Kidlington**

| | |
|---|---|
| Ben Edwards (9) | 163 |
| Eleanor O'Malley (10) | 164 |
| Daniel Murray (9) | 165 |
| Lonpe Adeniran (10) | 166 |
| Megan Keates (10) | 167 |
| Shannon O'Malley (10) | 168 |
| George Young (10) | 169 |
| Rachel O'Mahoney (10) | 170 |
| Samuel Hazell (9) | 171 |
| Kiana Bamdad (10) | 172 |
| Oliver Clark (9) | 173 |
| Katie Smith (9) | 174 |
| Olivia Pickford (9) | 175 |
| Bethany Cattell (10) | 176 |
| Jessica Featherstone (10) | 177 |

**Thomas A Becket Middle School, Worthing**

| | |
|---|---|
| Eco-School Reps (8-12 yrs) | 178 |

**Vale First & Middle School, Worthing**

| | |
|---|---|
| Natalya Fisher  (8) | 179 |
| Jessica Jackman  (10) | 180 |
| Lucy Piper  (10) | 181 |
| Emma Duncan  (8) | 182 |
| Ben Colburn  (8) | 183 |
| Matthew Votta  (7) | 184 |
| Georgia Smith  (8) | 185 |
| Amy Little  (8) | 186 |
| Max Tozer  (8) | 187 |
| Jamie Ward  (8) | 188 |
| Meredith Furlong  (8) | 189 |
| Fay Mugridge  (8) | 190 |
| Chloe Honess  (10) | 191 |
| Lauren McIlrath  (7) | 192 |
| Jack Cannon  (8) | 193 |
| Hannah Potiphar  (9) | 194 |
| Bethany Moxham  (9) | 195 |
| Lara Miles  (9) | 196 |
| Minni Whiffen  (8) | 197 |
| Brae Parker  (8) | 198 |
| Carrie Dollner  (9) | 199 |
| Katherine Scott  (9) | 200 |
| Lauryn Cook  (8) | 201 |
| Jodie Ward  (9) | 202 |
| Francesca Collier  (8) | 203 |
| Harvey Newman  (9) | 204 |
| Lois Bevan  (10) | 205 |
| Caroline Birch  (10) | 206 |

# The Poems

## Recycling Must Be Good

Recycling is very good,
Better use of items.
Recycling must be good,
It saves tons of energy.

Recycling is very good,
It stops us wasting it all.
Recycling must be good,
It teaches us a lesson.

But I'll tell you what,
Recycling must be good.
Never throw away one thing
Because there is no other way.

**Thomas Baker (10)**
**Brentwood Prep School, Brentwood**

# Recycling Poem

R ecycling is a great idea.
E lectricity can be saved.
C ycling instead of driving will help too!
Y ou could help the world if you recycle.
C 'mon and help the world be a better place.
L ittering is wrong and you shouldn't do it.
E very day we could be saving lots of things.

**Inigo Taylor (10)**
**Brentwood Prep School, Brentwood**

## Homeless People

Making the world a better place would protect our big nation,
Throughout the homeless and all the poor, who throw litter away
                                            then eat them raw.
The tramps that live on cardboard go wandering down the street,
Always begging for money and looking for something to eat.
When I walk past I feel very sick to see where these people lay,
So get rid of these bugs and stop all these thugs, who are ruining
                                            this world today.

**Edward Marling (10)**
**Brentwood Prep School, Brentwood**

## Being Homeless

H omeless is disaster
O ver the world
M ore people are dying
E verybody is hungry
L ots of people can be saved
E verybody help to
S ave the people
S ave the world.

**Matthew Perry (10)**
Brentwood Prep School, Brentwood

## Global Warming

Do you like tigers?
I do.
Do you turn off electricity when you stop using it?
I do.
Do you care about the environment?
I do.
Do you care about the ice caps melting?
I do.

Well then, if you do please try to do something about it!
I do.

**Fleur Sumption (10)**
**Brentwood Prep School, Brentwood**

## Global Warming! Stop It!

We have to stop global warming,
It's starting loads of floods!
We have to stop global warming,
Or say bye to polar bear cubs!

We have to stop global warming
And save all polar bears!
We have to stop global warming,
It's giving me nightmares!

We have to stop global warming,
We have to solve this case!
We have to stop global warming
And make the world a better place!

**Lily Ball (10)**
**Brentwood Prep School, Brentwood**

## Homelessness

Homeless people are starving,
Dying every day,
Begging for money,
Sleeping on the streets,
Always lonely,
Often cold and wet,
Not thought about enough
By us.

**Hannah Barnbrook (9)**
**Brentwood Prep School, Brentwood**

## Homeless People

Thunder clapping,
Hungry people,
All wandering round streets,
Poor and scared,
Lonely and hungry,
Begging for food,
Begging for clothes,
Cardboard boxes for sleeping,
Paper for sitting,
Why do people ignore and laugh?
Not thinking about how they would cope.
Hungry, scared and worried,
Do you?

**Kimia Khorshid (9)**
**Brentwood Prep School, Brentwood**

# War

War is very woeful
And people are hopeful
That the war will stop.
If countries make peace with each other,
Nobody will have to go to war with one another.
There is the navy, army and the RAF,
Sometimes causes death,
So I hope the war will stop.
If I was president,
I would make a new law,
It would be no war,
So I hope the war will stop.

**Ryan Norman (10)**
**Brentwood Prep School, Brentwood**

## Extinction Of Animals

Why do we kill them?
Coats and bags, shoes and food,
Animals don't kill us so they can wear skin.
Some animals are extinct because their habitat is being cut down.
Some are just being killed.
We can't help animals that die because of diseases,
But what we can help with,
We should help with,
*We can help animals*
*So we should.*

**Sara Linney (10)**
**Brentwood Prep School, Brentwood**

## The Big Green Saving Machine

R emember
E very
C an
Y ou
C lean and
L eave in recycling bin
I s made into
N ew metal
G ood for the environment.

**Ben Hazlewood (8)**
**Churcham Primary School, Churcham**

## Homeless

Being homeless is very sad.
Littering things is very bad.
The storms are around there is nowhere to go.
When people die it is as sad as you know.
Eco-people are very good helping me and helping you.
We help you as much as we can,
Keeping you safe and giving you food and water as well.

**Katie Hyett (8)**
**Churcham Primary School, Churcham**

## Rainforest

If we all put our heads together
We can save the world
And we can stop all our bad storms
We can blow them aside and say hello sun.

**Joseph Lunnon (11)**
**Churcham Primary School, Churcham**

## War And Disease

W here are all the animals?
A re they near extinction?
R eally you could help the world today.

A penny could help charity to save people's lives,
N ever say you cannot help because you could.
D id you know you could help millions of people?

D o you want to save the world?
I do so much,
S ee if your penny doesn't help others,
E verything helps,
A ll people say they can't, but they can.
S ave lives.
E very person could do their bit!

**Warren Greaves (8)**
**Churcham Primary School, Churcham**

## The Big Green Poetry Machine

H elp children with no water,
E ither send water pumps or give them,
A ll children should have water,
L et children express their feelings,
T ake water to African children,
H elp the Third World!

**Oliver Snell (8)**
**Churcham Primary School, Churcham**

## Save The World

R emember to put it in the bin.
E vents show it helps us all.
C ans can go in a recycling bin.
Y ou can help the world survive.
C an you walk to put it in the bin?
L ives lie in our hands.
I put the can in the bin and the world comes back again.
N ature relies on us . . .
G et a box and put cans, paper and all sorts of things in.

*Recycling!*

**Emily Arkell (9)**
**Churcham Primary School, Churcham**

## Litter

L et's put our litter in the bin.
I nstead of throwing it on the floor, throw it in the bin.
T ake your litter home or in a bin, but not on the floor.
T ake your litter with you until you find a bin.
E veryone can help.
R ecycle your litter!

**Harriet Price (8)**
**Churcham Primary School, Churcham**

## You Can Make A Difference

D on't leave rubbish on the floor
I t is bad to chop trees down.
S top now! You can make a difference.
E veryone can make a difference.
A nimals die from litter.
S ave the planet now.
E veryone can help,we need me and you now.

**Georgia Matthews (9)**
**Churcham Primary School, Churcham**

## Rainforests

R ainforests are disappearing
A nimals are becoming extinct
I 'm really annoyed with this devastation
N ever before have trees fallen so rapidly . . .
F orests are falling
O ther machines are cutting down trees and disturbing
                                                animal habitats

R ecycle for rainforest
E njoy the rainforest; it's a natural habitat
S top cutting down trees
T urn cutting down trees into regeneration trees.

**Ben Fisher (9)**
**Churcham Primary School, Churcham**

# Environments

E nvironments are being destroyed.
N o more littering.
V ehicles are making the world burn.
I f we don't stop now the world will be destroyed.
R ivers are drying up.
O zone gases are coming through.
N o more landfills.
M ore bicycles should be made.
E veryone should recycle.
N ot enough bikes.
T he world will be destroyed.
S top famines, don't waste food.

**William Sekinger (10)**
Churcham Primary School, Churcham

## Save Our World

I love the world so much
But really it's out of touch.
Recycling we need to do
Pollution - it's not new.
Rainforests are being cut
Litter, I just tut!
Animals will just die -
Extinction . . . why?
Poverty just mean
War is just obscene!
Disease is spreading fast
Being homeless should not last

The world needs to be saved!

**Adam Rees (11)**
**Churcham Primary School, Churcham**

## Rainforest

R ainforests I love
A rainforest will help us live
I n a rainforest there's lots of birds
N ear to the rainforest there's a waterfall
F lowing water dashes through the rainforest
O ver the rainforest it looks so fresh
R aindrops falling down in spots on your head
E veryone can hear the animals and birds
S ome animals might be up high and some low
T ime to time the monkeys swing.

**Alannah Hyett (10)**
**Churcham Primary School, Churcham**

## Say No! To Pollution

P ollution ruins our world,
O il, gas, rubbish, fumes
L ittered around our planet,
L ike a label, labelling our world - *danger!*
U tterly terrible!
T ime is running out.
I f we're going to save
O ur world say
N o to pollution - *now!*

**Alexander Brett (8)**
**Dame Bradbury's School, Saffron Walden**

# War

W ar is bad
A ll of you stop wasting your lives
R un to save the world

K illing is bad
I f this carries on we will all die
L ight up your lives
L et war stop
S o don't let me down. Stop!

**Martin John Booyens (8)**
**Dame Bradbury's School, Saffron Walden**

## Poverty

P oor, poor homeless people,
O ne mattress between 10,
V omit on the floor,
E aten mouldy bread scattered around,
R uined lives,
T atty clothes,
Y oung people crying.

M essy homes on the street,
A bandoned people all around,
K icking babies screaming,
E nvy poverty.

A ngry government make a change to poverty.

C ome on government,
H and over power to homeless people,
A round the world poverty spreads,
N o more people will be homeless,
G o on change it,
E veryone will be happy now.

**Katie Rushton (9)**
**Dame Bradbury's School, Saffron Walden**

# Racism

R acism's wrong everyone knows
A lways be kind to people with different skin
C olour doesn't matter, it's how you feel
I t's really bad what people say
S it them down, push it out of your mind
M an, just sit them down, get it out of your head.

**William Palmer (9)**
**Dame Bradbury's School, Saffron Walden**

## Helpless, Homeless

Helpless, homeless on the floor,
Helpless, homeless till no more,
Help the homeless on the street,
They need more,
Give them a treat!

Helpless, homeless needs somebody,
Helpless, homeless, pleads for more
Helpless, homeless on the floor,
Helpless, homeless has no more,
Helpless, homeless, how would you feel?
Helpless, homeless,
Helpless, homeless.

**Francesca Simmons**
**Dame Bradbury's School, Saffron Walden**

## Endangered Animals

Endangered animals getting shot,
Hunters shooting, killing. Animals dying,
They have as much right to live here as we do,
Cute as a newborn baby if you look carefully,
Please just stop,
I think it's as cruel as killing us,
Endangered animals,
Horrid, ugly hunters!

**Harriet Lander (9)**
**Dame Bradbury's School, Saffron Walden**

## Animals Are Dying

A nimals are dying
N ight and day they're not surviving
I nuits kill polar bears
M ankind might pollute the world
A fter we have gone away
L ight or dark there'll be no movement
S unshine may bring a fly or two.

A nimals are not surviving
R ecycling is something to do to help
E nvironment is losing out.

D ying deer is a bad sign
Y oung animals have no chance to survive
I gloos are all slush
N ight and day it's getting hotter
G lobal warming's coming faster.

**Maddy Ball (9)**
**Dame Bradbury's School, Saffron Walden**

## Homeless Child In Burma

A child in Burma, after the big wave.
Sadly searching for her family.
Ragged clothes, dark skin, brown hair.
Like an animal that lives on its own.
A child is as fragile as a wine glass.
She is lonely and very sad.
No one to care for her.
She reminds me of a heart broken into two.

**Olivia Richardson (9)**
**Dame Bradbury's School, Saffron Walden**

## War Is Bad, Stop It

W ar should not happen
A ll people die
R apid and wild

I t goes on for years
S leeping there, eating there

B ad people should stop
A fter war families are sad
D ead, people would not be if you did something

S tay at home, don't go
T oo many people die
O ff you go, save the world for us
P eople might help if you help

I f I help can you help?
T o save the world from misery.

**Euan Buchanan (9)**
**Dame Bradbury's School, Saffron Walden**

## If I Was An Animal

I f I was an animal
F lying high
I t would be wonderful to see green trees

W here would I live if there were none?
A bove a cloud in the sky
S oaring high above the sky I want to see green trees

A nimals die, people cry
N o animals left except me and you

A nimals should be happy
N ever never sad
I n the air, on the ground
M ost animals
A ll animals should be happy
L eave behind all the bad and bring back all the good!

**Ella Horwell (9)**
**Dame Bradbury's School, Saffron Walden**

# War

War, war oh how dreadful it is
War, war people will die
War, war I hate it, do you?
War, war people starve
War, war even more people die
War, war people get forced to fight

Will it ever end?

**Ben James (8)**
**Dame Bradbury's School, Saffron Walden**

# Poetry

Poetry machine
We all love the scene
So why don't you come play with me?
And come and see what the world can be
Don't drive, cycle
Don't throw rubbish away, recycle
We can change the world into a different place
Only if we change it from this awful disgrace.

**Oliver Snell (9)**
**Dame Bradbury's School, Saffron Walden**

# Climate Change - Haikus

Climate change is bad
Climate change ruins our ice
We have to change now

You have to act now
The world will be flooded soon
Don't ever waste time

Our world is dying
Don't waste your time pondering
Save our planet now!

Recycle, reuse
Walk, cycle or use the bus
Shape up all of us.

**Ethan Monks (9)**
**Dame Bradbury's School, Saffron Walden**

## Animals

Animals are dying, birds will stop flying.
The rainforest is crying, crashing to the floor,
animals are dying even more!
Pollution and litter aren't going well,
more animals are getting ill,
but now we are helping animals survive.
Hopefully animals will get better and stay alive!

If we recycle our rubbish we can save our trees,
the animals won't die of disease.
If we turn off our switches and refuse our bags,
it will help the climate so the animals can relax!

**Lucy Clements (9)**
**Dame Bradbury's School, Saffron Walden**

## Ill

you need a pill,
you need to get better,
ill you need some medicine.

rashes and fevers,
are types of illness,
may need to see a doctor.

If you're ill help is needed,
Please help people who are ill!

**Louis Bartlett (9)**
**Dame Bradbury's School, Saffron Walden**

# Litter

Litter, litter
It's very bitter
To put litter on the floor

Cans, cans
Ban the cans on the floor
Oh yes, ban the cans on the floor

Wrappers, wrappers
No more wrappers anymore
Don't put wrappers on the floor

Bins, bins
Put it in
No more litter on the floor

Recycle, recycle
Let's all recycle
No more litter anymore.

**Oliver Turpin (9)**
**Dame Bradbury's School, Saffron Walden**

## Death Of The Dodo

'Dodo why did you die?
Was it just because you could not fly?'
'No, I was hunted for my meat and fat,
They chopped down the jungle, my only habitat.'
'Dodo, that's so unfair,
We must protect our land, sea and air.'
'My island was an ocean jewel,
How could you humans be so cruel?'
'Dodo you definitely did not deserve it,
Our planet is precious, we must conserve it.'

**Andrew Williams (9)**
**Dame Bradbury's School, Saffron Walden**

# Extinction! - Haikus

What is extinction?
When animals live no more.
Here are examples.

A wild dinosaur!
The tyrannosaurus rex.
Big meat-eating teeth.

Platybelodon!
A large, long-mouthed elephant.
Except with small ears.

The big-tusked mammoth!
They were hunted for their meat,
Also for their fur.

Sabre-tooth tiger!
A ferocious-looking beast.
Big teeth hanging down.

There is a saying,
'You're as dead as a dodo'.
Dodos have strong beaks.

The dodo was slow.
Sailors killed them for their food.
They were easy prey.

The quagga died out
In year 1870.
They were a zebra.

Types of frogs have died
Because of men cutting trees
In the rainforests.

Now the white rhino.
Please save them from extinction.
Only thirty left.

**Plum Thatcher (9)**
**Dame Bradbury's School, Saffron Walden**

## Trees

Trees, trees they help you breathe.
They help you breathe, breathe, breathe.

Sometimes they can die,
Sometimes they can cry.

Trees can sway, when you say yay,
So can you all say, a big yay!

Trees, trees they help you breathe,
They help you breathe all day.

Trees can sway when you say yay,
So let's all say a big *hooray!*

**Laura Cox (9)**
**Dame Bradbury's School, Saffron Walden**

## Litter

Litter here, litter there, litter, litter everywhere.
In the Thames, on the street,
There's loads of litter at our feet.
Plastic bags hanging in trees,
That can't be good for the birds or bees.
Oh no! Who's dropped that can?
Oh good here comes the garbage man.
All this trash has taken up so much room,
We really need a great big broom.
Remember we can all do our bit,
So make sure you recycle it!
Plastic, paper and even tin
Can be processed and used again.
If I could have just one wish
It would be to make a law of *no more rubbish!*

**Cameron Lewis (9)**
**Dame Bradbury's School, Saffron Walden**

## Animals That Are Endangered

E agle moves but still gets shot.
N o one seems to care.
D odos gone forever.
A nother species down the drain.
N early all the white rhinos extinct.
G orillas fought their way back.
E lephants are killed for their tusks.
R ed kangaroos are getting run over.
E very Siberian tiger should be worried.
D estroying the rainforest destroys animals' homes.

**Josie Taylor (9)**
**Dame Bradbury's School, Saffron Walden**

## Why War?

War, war, war!
All we hear, war here, war there.
It's so scary, guns' noise.
*Bang! Bang! Bang!* All dead.

Why fight? Why kill?
Why even bother killing men?

What if it happened here?
People wasting their lives.
People being selfish, taking land, not sharing.
Burning houses falling to the ground.
Just fighting for a bit of cash.
All the time people dying for a country.
Sadness for many families crying in the night.

**Ryan Spencer (9)**
**Dame Bradbury's School, Saffron Walden**

## Trigger

One little finger on the trigger,
If you get the aim right,
One little movement,
One man gone
And this movement will
Change your life forever
And lose a soul,
So avoid the kill.

**Sam Featherstone (9)**
**Dame Bradbury's School, Saffron Walden**

# Animal Extinction

E very animal was different, some would purr and some had fur,
X -rays showed the way they were.
T oday we try to save them all,
I n zoos and cages, no matter how small.
N ow it's time to take more care,
C os if we don't they won't be there.
T -rex, dodo, quagga to name a few,
I t's for sure you'll never see them in a zoo.
O ur environment we must protect,
N ow or never, no way we can quit.

**Olivia Ross-Adams (8)**
**Dame Bradbury's School, Saffron Walden**

## Poor Animals

It really is not fiction
That some animals are close to extinction.
A Sumatran tiger and a polar bear,
Are gradually becoming quite rare.
The poor tigers are being sold,
Whilst the rich men are gaining gold.
The melting of the Arctic ice
Is making us pay the price.
We are adding to the pollution,
So we must find a solution.
We must be over fishing
Because the whales and sharks are going missing.
We should be feeling emotion
Because of the warming of the ocean.
The king penguins will be affected
And that was unexpected.
So as you can see
It's up to you and me,
To protect the animals
On land and in the sea.

**Elizabeth Curno  (9)**
**Great Berry Primary School, Basildon**

## Serious Warning!

Global warming is really bad,
And when I think of it, it makes me sad.

I always turn the light off, then it's too dark,
But how do I stop an oil spill that kills a baby shark?

I really try to recycle in bags coloured pink,
You have to wash the cans out or else they'll really stink.

To save using up petrol, Dad he does slow down,
When someone drives by really fast, it actually makes him frown.

There are many bad things that make global warming
And we should listen carefully and understand the serious warning!

**Michael Burdett (10)**
**Great Berry Primary School, Basildon**

## Litter - Haikus

Litter everywhere,
Do the people really care!
Green land is quite rare.

We need to clean up,
Put your rubbish in the bin,
Recycle as well.

**Emma Jane Gadsdon (10)**
**Great Berry Primary School, Basildon**

## What A World
*(Inspired by 'What a Wonderful World' by Louis Armstrong)*

I see skies of smoke,
Dead roses too,
Brown, brown trees,
For me and you
And I think to myself,
*What a horrible world.*

There were clouds of white,
Sky so blue
And trees so green
For me and you,
And I think to myself,
*'Twas a beautiful world.*

**Âine Griffiths (9)**
**Great Berry Primary School, Basildon**

## Zimbabwe

I, me, Harry Browse,
Want to stop wars and rows.
For my treacherous transmission
I've entered a competition.
For instance take Zimbabwe,
Ruled by the horrible Mugabe.
Wars and deaths he set apart,
I feel like a knife's through my back,
A spear's through my heart.
Sometimes I think the man shouldn't live!
But what is violence going to give?
Do you wish the world can be
Free of deaths and poverty?
I hope my message has come across,
To all the people who've had that loss.

**Harry Browse (10)**
**Great Berry Primary School, Basildon**

## Don't Be A Litterbug!

Don't be a litterbug
Don't be someone bad
Don't be dropping litter
Or you'll make me sad

Don't be a litterbug
Don't be nasty
Don't be a litterbug
Or the world will be ghastly

Don't be a litterbug
Don't be horrible
Don't be a litterbug
Or the world will be unbearable.

**Chloe Harvey (10)**
**Great Berry Primary School, Basildon**

## The Senses

*I see:*

Rubbish piling up, landfill sites overflowing,
Sealife dying, their waters poisoned by our disregard,
Gases filling the air, grey clouds swelling,
Ice caps diminishing, seas rising, destruction and extinction abound.

*I feel:*

Sad that the sky's full of grey, I can't see the stars,
Bad, as this is what the world is like,
Angry, as people are selfish, not caring enough to make a difference,
Helpless - when will this end?

*I hear:*

Loud music pumping, I need to sleep,
Lawnmowers roaring, workmen's tools screaming,
Car horns blaring, sirens screeching,
Helicopters and planes buzzing by.

*I smell:*

Fossil fuels burning,
Coal, oil and gas creating thick plumes of grey smoke,
Exhaust fumes filling the air, cars going by without a second thought,
Barbecues cooking, sizzling through the air.

*I taste:*

Bad things in my mouth when I think about pollution,
Bitterness that we are not caring enough to do more,
Sadness that my children's children's Earth is slowly being destroyed.

*I believe:*

That *our* Earth can be a better place,
We need to keep on caring and keep on protecting.

*Love your Earth!*

**Erin Mollie Rose Draper (9)**
**Great Berry Primary School, Basildon**

## Litterbugs

There are people in the world that think it's OK to drop litter.
This makes me very cross, angry and bitter.
When I walk down the street, all I seem to meet, is the rubbish under my feet.
Chewing gum on the floor is very sticky, when I try to get it off it's very tricky.
Crisp packets, chocolate wrappers and fast food bags, I think it's really gross looking at old smelly fags.
Drink cans and plastic bottles really make my mind boggle,
Why did that person chuck it on the ground, because in the bin it's safe and sound.
Dog walkers should be more aware when cleaning up the poop, it doesn't take a lot to use a poopy scoop.

So if we all work together, whatever the weather, pick up that rubbish you dropped on the floor, it's not that much of a boring chore.
Then our pavements, parks and roads will be nice and cleaner,
Think about the world we live in and be a whole lot *greener.*

**Emily Morgan (9)**
**Great Berry Primary School, Basildon**

## Recycling

Plastic, paper, bottles and tins,
Please don't throw it in the bins,
It causes global warming
And stops the ozone layer from forming.
Recycle your waste
Without any haste,
Let's all look after this planet together
And we will have a safe world forever.

**Bayley Archer (10)**
**Great Berry Primary School, Basildon**

# War

What is the point of war?
They are really bad.
What are we fighting for?
Has the world gone mad?
Lots of blood is shed,
Lots of people dead.
What's the point of war?
What are we fighting for?

**Samuel Thomas (9)**
**Great Berry Primary School, Basildon**

## Understanding

Do you want to live under a clear blue sky or do you want to die?
The solution is clear. Stop the pollution.

Stop the litter, just recycle, poverty, racism, disease and war,
Pick out one that's knocking on your door.

Animals, trees and even people need shelter, love
                                            and understanding.

**Kennedy Gorrie (9)**
**Great Berry Primary School, Basildon**

## Stop The War

Stop the war
For people are poor
They'll have nowhere to live
But you can give
Stop the fighting
For people are dying
The bombs are dropping
As people are sobbing
Stop the hate
For people should be mates
People are screaming
When people should be believing
Stop the fire
For people desire
Start the peace
So people are free.

**Faye Schuster (10)**
**Great Berry Primary School, Basildon**

## Rainforests

R ainforest, rainforest
A great place of beauty
I declare
N ever cut down trees
F or everyone on this planet
O pen your eyes
R ainforest, rainforest
E veryone try your best to
S ave the species of the rainforest
T rees are the lungs of the world
S ave our Earth for a brighter future!

**Hannah Mathieson-Cheater (10)**
Great Berry Primary School, Basildon

## Pollution, Pollution

Pollution, pollution, it's a terrible thing,
The cars and the boats and the aeroplanes polluting every day.
It's not good for me or you.
Nobody likes pollution, no, no, no they don't.
We need beautiful fresh air,
Lovely clean water and much, much more beautiful, clean things.
The cars and the planes pollute the air
And the boats pollute the water.
No, no, no, make it stop.

**Megan Kendrick (10)**
**Great Berry Primary School, Basildon**

## Help! - Haiku

Please help save the world
And clear up all our litter
Save our animals.

**Jennifer Munro (10)**
**Great Berry Primary School, Basildon**

## Global Warming

The world is dying away
Getting worse day after day
Polar bears losing their homes
There will never be anymore snow
Global warming will affect us all
No more snow will be there to fall
Icebergs melting into the sea
This isn't the way the world should be
Rivers rising, flooding towns
No more smiles, only frowns
Global warming will affect us all
I don't like this, not at all.

**Lucia Freeman (10)**
**Great Berry Primary School, Basildon**

## Litterbugs

Litter, litter everywhere
Every table, every chair
On the floor stop your grin
And just put it in the bin

It's bad a lot, for me and you
And do you know what animals do?
They eat it and die
And sadly float up in the sky

When you're out and feeling flirty
Don't drop litter 'cause you'll look dirty
So please stop littering
And put your rubbish in the bin.

**Phoebe Peters (9)**
**Great Berry Primary School, Basildon**

## Litter

Litter, litter everywhere,
People drop it, they don't care.
There is a crisp packet, a plastic cup,
But someone has to clean it up.
Metal, paper, rubber, tin,
Just put your rubbish in the bin.
Litter, litter everywhere.

**Toby Callaghan (9)**
**Great Berry Primary School, Basildon**

## Litter

L itter is terrible for the environment
I f we all recycle our world would be greener
T hink before you throw that item away
T here are many things you can recycle
E veryday things like cans, paper, tins and so much more
R ecycling is such a small part but makes a big difference.

**Nicholas Like (10)**
**Great Berry Primary School, Basildon**

# Litter

I open my eyes and all I can see
Is litter, litter, litter.
Litter is everywhere you go
Every place
Every town
Grubby and disgusting
I hate litter
For how does litter get everywhere?
Us people
I and everyone else can't stand litter
*We hate litter.*

**Erica Wilks (9)**
**Great Berry Primary School, Basildon**

## The World

The world from a distance looks all blue and green,
But if you look closer there's much more to be seen.
With beautiful oceans as blue as the sky,
Big towering mountains way up high.
There's all sorts of creatures under our seas
And wonderful forests all full of trees.
It looks so beautiful so keep it that way
By looking after it each and every day.

**Emily Lizzimore (9)**
**Great Berry Primary School, Basildon**

## Don't Drop It

Drop it,
Stop it,
Pick it up,
Put it in a bin,
Make the world a tidy place,
For us to all live in!

Please don't drop your rubbish,
When you're out 'n' about,
Because we all don't want you to be
A lazy litter lout!

**Amy McMillan (9)**
**Great Berry Primary School, Basildon**

## Pollution

We have a beautiful world
That is suffering
It's destroying our future.

**Kwabena Adu-Poku (10)**
Great Berry Primary School, Basildon

## To Save Our Planet

Try tigers, lions, monkeys
And camels with big humpies,
Killing animals doesn't make you grown up,
It just makes you get bad luck.
As soon as you make the difference,
It's us, we don't get the appearance
To save our planet,
Don't kill the maggots.
So help us, we need your help,
The birds, animals, trees,
Please, they help us breathe.
We have to hear their cheeps,
So please don't eat meat.
So save the planet
Don't kill maggots,
Or animals will become extinct.

**Claire Poulter (9)**
**Great Berry Primary School, Basildon**

# War

W oeful war
A re you OK?
R emain unseen and safe.

**Tom England (9)**
**Great Berry Primary School, Basildon**

## Extinction

Homes being destroyed
Being hunted and trapped
How long have they got?

Will there be any left
For future generations,
Animals and birds?

**Joseph Dulieu-Hasler (10)**
**Great Berry Primary School, Basildon**

# Reduce, Reuse, Recycle

Reduce, reuse, recycle.
Reduce, reuse, recycle,
Or everyone will be crying,
Whilst all the trees are dying.

Reduce, reuse, recycle,
Reduce, reuse, recycle,
Or the polar bears will be dying
Because they've lost their homes.

Reduce, reuse, recycle,
Reduce, reuse, recycle,
Because it's not fantastic
To throw away your plastic.

We must find a solution
To all of Man's pollution
And the only way is to
Reduce, reuse, recycle.

**Jonathon Bartlett (10)**
**Great Berry Primary School, Basildon**

## Life On The Streets

Bottles, jars, paper and soil
All our life we live in toil
Waste, waste, waste, waste
With nothing nice for us to taste

We sleep in boxes all around town
Hoping, praying
We don't get knocked down

Surviving on the streets
Believe me is no fun
All the young people carrying guns
When will we work as one?

**Stacey O'Connor (10)**
**Great Berry Primary School, Basildon**

## Zog The Little Green Frog

Hi there, my name is Zoggy, my friends call me Zog.
I live in the rainforest, I am a little green tree frog.
My skin is bright green and my eyes are deep red,
If something isn't done soon me and my rainforest neighbours will all be dead.
The rainforest is quiet and safe and has no traffic,
You may have seen it in National Geographic.
I can hop to the stream, I need to keep my skin wet
Because if I get ill I can't visit a vet.
My mum and dad keep telling me to be careful,
They say it's a jungle out there,
There are a lot of strange creatures here, in fact they're quite rare,
But the strangest creature of all walks on two legs,
I think they're called Man,
He is not here for the weather, to get a good tan,
Oh no he is here to cut the trees down, the place I call home,
Without my tree I will become homeless.
My simple life has become a complete mess,
Man cuts down the trees to make room for farming,
At this rate it's rather alarming.
Paper and timber are made from the tree,
They are loaded onto lorries and put on ships and cross the sea.
The wood is processed into paper, they all seem to use it,
Printing off junk mail and email, Man really abuses it.
The more they use the more they need,
It's in Man's DNA, they survive on greed.
So next time you log on and need to print,
Remember Zog the little green frog, he may have become extinct.

**Matthew Deaville (10)**
Great Berry Primary School, Basildon

## What Did I Do?

L ife is an excellent thing and I'm ruining it by throwing rubbish
<br>on the floor
I t's not good what I'm doing because I sue cars every day
T he birds are dying and the skies are going black
T he trees are dying as well with the birds, it's like the world
<br>is in a sack
E lephants eat vegetables and grass so they might be in
<br>for extinction
R ed rosy apples all bruised and black, what did I do to make
<br>the world sad?

**Samuel Baughan (10)**
Great Berry Primary School, Basildon

## Litter

L itter
I take care to
T hrow away
T rash cans is where it should stay
E veryone knows what to do to
R ecycle!

**Jon Andrews (10)**
**Great Berry Primary School, Basildon**

## War, No Mercy

War should be no more!
But what is it for?
It demolishes buildings
And it kills the human race.
Oh no, somebody has attacked our base.
*Bang!* Another life is gone.
So what is the point if you break a joint?
And war is no good if you die with a thud
And that is why war should be no more.

**Zeeshan Rasool (10)**
**Great Berry Primary School, Basildon**

## Pollution

P ollution is terrible!
O ver 30 tons of rubbish is put in landfill sites per month!
L andfill pollutes!
L andfill is useless, so what's the point?
U s plus the world are unhappy with it!
T he time has come to do something about it!
I t's pathetic!
O h, how it must stop so . . .
*N o more pollution!*

**Michael Wright (10)**
**Great Berry Primary School, Basildon**

## Climate Change

C lean nice country.
L orries are causing a lot of pollution.
I nhibit pollution and save population.
M ake your future clean and nice.
A nimals are close to extinction so be wise.
T he world is not clean and nice, don't be mean.
E xpress your feelings for the world, don't just dream.

C lean the roads by picking litter.
H elps your community, better.
A n enormous change to the world.
N eed to keep the world clean for all.
G ain a better and cleaner future.
E nd all this pollution and let this world nurture.

**Daanish Ahmad (10)**
**Great Berry Primary School, Basildon**

## Anything That Harms Our Earth

Anything that harms our Earth
Pollution makes everything smell,
Including a tiny, tiny shell,
Get rid of the trains,
Cars, buses and planes,
If the rubbish dump gets bigger,
We might just need a great big digger,
But if we use the pink bags,
Nobody has to nag,
Because the rubbish will be all gone.

**Celine Vadher (10)**
**Great Berry Primary School, Basildon**

## Save Our Earth

Our Earth is so polluted,
So let's do somin' about it,
Let's stop this, stop this stupid war,
So why are we doin' it?
Let's stop killin' our Earth,
Let's be friends with our Earth
And don't kill it,
Our lovely, lovely Earth.

**Ross Pavelin (10)**
**Great Berry Primary School, Basildon**

## Plant A Tree

Two thirds of the world is water,
One third of the world is land,
Half of that third is forest and some of that is sand,
The world is a living thing,
With lungs that need to breathe,
The lungs are green with trunks of brown,
Covered all in leaves.
If you care about the climate, the world,
Or what's to be,
Then go outside, right now
And go and plant a tree!

**Georgia Chandler (10)**
**Great Berry Primary School, Basildon**

## Saving The World

No polluting, no polluting, you really need to recycle,
The world is at stake, the world is at stake, we really need your help.
Do not destroy the animals for their own sake,
Don't cut down the trees otherwise they won't have any eyes.
The war has begun,
Let's save our planet from being destroyed.
The Earth is getting more polluted,
We need to make the Earth a good place.

**Ryan Foss (9)**
**Great Berry Primary School, Basildon**

## Recycling For The World

We all need to work hard together,
Recycling will help global warming weather,
The people need to look after the planet,
Or we will all fry and the world will die.
Recycle your rubbish - it's not hard,
It's just your old clothes, papers,
Plastic, glass, grass and card.
*Please just do it - recycle!*

**Joe McKean (10)**
**Great Berry Primary School, Basildon**

## Untitled

Trees are green
The sky is blue
If you breathe in air it's good for you
Next time you're out breathing in air
Remember to keep your blood temperature fair
The wind breeze is soft and light
The trees will get darker
As you pass through the night.

**Courtney Treadwell**
**Great Berry Primary School, Basildon**

## Rubbish

Listen out for the rubbish bin
Hear a *ring, ring, ring* as you put the litter in,
No junk around is a hoot
When you throw rubbish in the garbage shoot
There's the binman in his orange suit
And his truck goes *toot, toot.*

**Luke Cullen (9)**
**Limes Farm Junior School, Chigwell**

## Keep Britain Tidy

I'm a piece of litter blowing down the street
Making it look untidy around people's feet.
Waiting for the dustman to come and clean the street,
Costing people money that they'd much rather keep.

**Charlotte Tillbrook (8)**
Limes Farm Junior School, Chigwell

# Litter

L itter is bad it makes me sad
I nstead of turning around and putting it on the ground
T hey should see a bin and put it in
T ogether we can change
E veryone of every age
R espect the land, we all need to make a stand.

**Paris-Jade Clarke-Brown (8)**
**Limes Farm Junior School, Chigwell**

## Change

Oh poor willow tree weep no more,
Sway with the gushing wind evermore,
Lighten faces with your green lively leaves,
Rain your beauty upon us.

Oh yet how my heart weeps
For all those lost souls washed away.
The storm so heartless and violent
Crushes all in its path.

What is life if people don't care?
How can you just look away?
Can you watch your loved ones fade away?
So just take a second to think and ask is this fair?
You can change the world today knowing there is a tomorrow.

**Naseema Khalique (11)**
**Limes Farm Junior School, Chigwell**

## Litter

Every morning when I see litter,
It makes the place smell rather bitter

And when I tell them to pick up
They leave their sweets and paper cups.

And then I went to look around,
I found rubbish no one else had found.

Next just remember, pick rubbish up this time,
Because this is why I wrote this rhyme.

**Naomi Alade (8)**
**Limes Farm Junior School, Chigwell**

## Recycle

Litter, litter all around,
I'm some litter on the ground,
Some litter down the street,
Sneaking under people's feet.
Recycle on the street,
That's what it's like being litter,
Going down the street.

**Ryan Snedker (9)**
**Limes Farm Junior School, Chigwell**

# Recycle

R ubbish goes in the bin
E co helps the environment
C ycle to school and work
Y ou should help the environment
C ycle back home
L ook after our world
E veryone should recycle their rubbish.

**Christopher Morris (8)**
**Longcot & Fernham CE Primary School, Longcot**

## Save Our Environment

E very animal needs care.
N o dropping litter everywhere.
V iolets and pansies will be gone if we don't help.
I nventions like cars will make the world sad.
R uining the world is really bad.
O tters won't play and foxes won't creep.
N o cheery animals fast sleep.
M echanical things like computers and TVs.
E nd the world and all its buzzy bees.
N o it wouldn't be good if we ruined the world.
T ry to be eco, save our *environment!*

**Holly Carlisle (9)**
Longcot & Fernham CE Primary School, Longcot

## Planet Pollution

Planet pollution is bad for us,
Traffic and cars and even a bus.
If you walk to school every day,
You'll be helping the world by the way!

When it is night take out all the plugs,
Then get into bed you'll be quite snug!
Nothing to worry about through the night,
No worrying about fires or lights.

Grow your own fruit for lunch,
Lovely apples that go *crunch, crunch!*
Dance about in the sun,
This is great, you'll be having some fun!

*Stop planet pollution!*

**Lucy Kent (9)**
**Longcot & Fernham CE Primary School, Longcot**

# We Can All Go Green

We can all go green as easy as it seems.
We can all go green as easy as we've seen,
By recycling all paper and turning off lights.

We can all go green as easy as it seems,
By reducing the amount of fires to reduce $CO_2$.

We can all go green as easy as it seems,
By throwing away the car keys and walking to school,
Raising the petrol prices and not burning oil,
Which all leads up to going eco.

**Luke Parry (8)**
**Longcot & Fernham CE Primary School, Longcot**

# The End

T he world is ending!
H elp save the world
E very can and bottle must be recycled

E arth is ending!
N ow recycle plastic
D o it and pollution will stop!

Countries are flooding
Save the world by walking to school
Please try not to be a fool.

Now you know how to save the world
Go and do it and don't waste time.

**Josh Sheppard (9)**
**Longcot & Fernham CE Primary School, Longcot**

# Recycle

R ecycle all the plastic you can
E verything recycled is fantastic
C ars can be made from your tins
Y ou need to put less in the bin
C ardboard, bottles and glass can all be recycled
L itter goes in the bin
E co-time save the world!

**Louise Jenkins (8)**
**Longcot & Fernham CE Primary School, Longcot**

# Rainforests

R ed squirrels are very rare.
A nimals need lots more care.
I f you cut down trees to make wooden combs.
N ow don't cut down animals' homes.
F orest floor has lots of bugs.
O nly silly people dig up all of the slugs.
R ed snakes won't eat.
E specially if it isn't meat.
S ave the animals and
T ogether we can
S *ave the rainforests!*

**Natasha Hingston (9)**
Longcot & Fernham CE Primary School, Longcot

# The Extinction

Animals are falling at a vast quantity,
This isn't a lie, it's the truth, it's reality.
Every three seconds an animal will die,
So listen to this message, it isn't a lie.
If you love animals you'll agree with me,
Go to the jungle and then you might see
How animals are dying, we've made them a mess,
Some are now homeless and being killed because of their stress.
Now you've read this message I repeat, it isn't a lie,
Now you know maybe the animals won't die!

**Georgia Stevens (11)**
**Longcot & Fernham CE Primary School, Longcot**

## War

War everybody has seen
War isn't calm and serene
War where people get killed
War where blood is spilled

War is blood and gore
War, cities will be destroyed
War where children are living in
War, a country has to win
War is blood and gore.

**Albert George Durham (10)**
**Longcot & Fernham CE Primary School, Longcot**

## Can We Do Anything?

Animals dying,
We are crying,
Especially in Beijing,
People chopping,
Trees dropping,
*Can we do anything?*

**Jenny Fotheringham (9)**
**Longcot & Fernham CE Primary School, Longcot**

## Animals Dying, Hear Them Crying

Animals dying, hear them crying,
with our hunting, we are killing them.
cutting down trees, destroying habitats,
endangered animals, extinct species.
Trapping them, choking them,
feeding their young litter.
Animals killed for tusks and skin.
Animals dying, hear them crying,
with our hunting, we are killing them.

**Yasmin Dowell (11)**
**Longcot & Fernham CE Primary School, Longcot**

# War

When countries fight,
it ends in war.
Soldiers risk their lives,
to sort out something of the government's doing.

Invading into countries,
killing innocent people,
that get involved in war,
when it is not their doing.

Disaster,
Devastation and
Destruction.

**Zoe Dowell (11)**
**Longcot & Fernham CE Primary School, Longcot**

## King Rats

Rats, rats they are so fat,
They will eat anything.
Litter is what they like best,
They will eat from the bin!

Rats are going to take over the world
With our litter!

**Joe Timms (11)**
**Longcot & Fernham CE Primary School, Longcot**

# Our World

Animals are dying
Extinction is coming
Litter everywhere
Pollution and war
But we can stop it
*Save the world!*

**William Casey (10)**
**Longcot & Fernham CE Primary School, Longcot**

## A Blanket Around The Earth

The Earth has a mum,
The ozone layer to be precise,
It looks after the world
And makes it very nice.

It takes away the bad things
And lets in the good things,
It makes a good shield,
But has never been revealed.

What are we doing?
We're destroying it quickly,
Making holes in our mum,
We are acting so dumb.

The Earth is getting warmer,
Scorching parks and fields,
We need our mum,
Someone protect us.

Eco-people we need you now,
Do something,
Anything,
*Please!*

**Jake Thacker-Pugsley (9)**
**Longcot & Fernham CE Primary School, Longcot**

## Good World Gone Bad

I am a fish, I live in the sea
please stop polluting it
because it's not fair on me.

I am a fox
I come out when it's late
please stop littering
because it can make me suffocate.

I am a bird
I live in a tree
please don't cut them down
because I will have to leave my family
*Please be green!*

**Kelsey-Louise Townsend (11)**
**Longcot & Fernham CE Primary School, Longcot**

## Being Homeless Isn't Fun

Being homeless isn't fun,
You live on the streets
And you have no money.
Please help the homeless,
We rummage through bins for food,
It's really annoying when we're not allowed in shops,
Nobody cares for us,
They just walk past us,
We don't have any friends,
We always beg for money,
We're sad because we are cold,
We sleep in a cardboard box,
That's uncomfy.

**Jess Brader (10)**
**Longcot & Fernham CE Primary School, Longcot**

# Rainforest

The rainforest is a beautiful place,
but not anymore.

When people came
the rainforest was changed.

Trees were cut down
and animals lost their homes.

So everybody out there,
please stop and think about
what you are doing!

**Matthew Owens (10)**
**Longcot & Fernham CE Primary School, Longcot**

## The Village Disappears

The people are very worried,
The ice caps are melting,
The water is coming,
Soon the village will disappear.

People are rushing around,
They need to get away soon,
They are going to lose their homes,
It is all because of us.

**Samuel Cooper (10)**
**Longcot & Fernham CE Primary School, Longcot**

## Kind Person

Litter picker-upper
Car stopper
Shelter giver
Food giver
Water lover
Non-smoker
Sea sailor.

**Adam Rich (11)**
**Longcot & Fernham CE Primary School, Longcot**

## Dear Humans

I am the fox and I am in grief,
You pollute our land right down to the ocean reefs.

You chop down the woods
And force other animals to leave,
They fly and crawl down the path
And bunch together and bustle and heave.

You hunt us down with hounds and horses
And won't leave us alone until death.
You fire your big guns at us
And never stop,
Then you leave us in a big mess.

**Alice Keegan (10)**
**Longcot & Fernham CE Primary School, Longcot**

## Tigers

Tigers are dying every day just for fur clothes,
Dying for no reason, everybody knows,
But no one does anything about it,
That's what makes me sad,
This is what we need to do to stop the bad,
So we need to protect these creatures
And save all their features,
We need to save tiger kind,
If you wouldn't mind.

**Hannah Laura Jones (10)**
**Longcot & Fernham CE Primary School, Longcot**

## Pollution, Pollution, Pollution!

Pollution packs the air,
Pollution crams the sea,
Pollution is getting so disastrous,
Eco-warriors are going to conclude it,
I can guarantee!

**George Timms (10)**
**Longcot & Fernham CE Primary School, Longcot**

## Dead Animals

We're killing all the animals,
by leaving litter everywhere.
All the animals are dying
and we are not aware.
We're using them to make things,
that sometimes we don't need,
we need to reduce animal killing
and we need to do it with speed.
We need to save the world,
let's hope we're not too late,
if we keep wasting energy,
we could destroy a whole state.

**Richard Cole (11)**
**Longcot & Fernham CE Primary School, Longcot**

# Poverty

Disgusting but deliberate,
How do they live with it?
Getting kicked and hit,
Being black, what's wrong with it?

Fighting is frightening,
The guns are like lightning,
Getting injured and robbed,
Then they lose their job.

No food, no water,
No shelter to house your daughter.

These people live in poverty,
Where can they flee?
These people are refugees,
How can we help with poverty?

**Natascha Blesing (11)**
Longcot & Fernham CE Primary School, Longcot

## Save Us

Elephants, polar bears, pandas and gorillas,
Us humans are all their killers,
Elephants' tusks, gorillas' skin,
Next I will be in a trash bin,
They've chopped our trees,
Those poor chimpanzees.

**Georgina Elbrow (10)**
**Longcot & Fernham CE Primary School, Longcot**

## Fishes In The Sea

I am a fish,
In the sea,
Swimming round,
Finding nets,
That fishers leave,
They're trying to catch us,
Going one by one,
Are all of us going,
Or will they stop
Catching us,
Eating us?
I feel like
I'm the last one left,
There's a net,
I've been caught.

**Kayleigh Booth (11)**
**Longcot & Fernham CE Primary School, Longcot**

## Stop Killing Animals

I am a bird, I live in a tree
Always was as can be
Horrible people cutting down trees
Will someone help me, please, please, please?

I am a fox, I live in a den
I am worried, again and again
My cubs eat litter you throw around
Please think about what you throw on the ground.

I am a deer, I live in the wood
Stop killing us, do you think you should?
All my fellow friends are dying
I hope some of you are sat there sighing.

We help stop animal cruelty,
Will you?

**William Peregrine (10)**
**Longcot & Fernham CE Primary School, Longcot**

## Litter Makes Pollution

Litter makes pollution, they do not mix.
It makes my heart beat 2-4-6.
Everyone should recycle their tins and cans.
Recycle your waste and look after your land.
Animals and plants will suffer, the rivers and seas.
Our world needs love and care, God put us here.
Remember these words and we will be fine,
It makes my heart beat 3-6-9 . . .

**Oliver Bolton (11)**
**Mountnessing Primary School, Mountnessing**

## Save The Rainforest

Jaguar, jaguar, look up there,
Monkeys, monkeys, everywhere!
Then come the people, *chop, chop, chop,*
Down fall the trees, the whole lot!

> Parrot, parrot, in trees green,
> They didn't know that you had seen,
> Your monkey friends fall to the ground,
> And you flew off safe and sound,
> Before your tree crashed to the ground.

Tiger, tiger in tall grass,
You decided to let them pass.
When they'd passed, you ran out,
To meet a pack of hunters stout.

> Monkey, monkey, chattering with glee,
> You didn't know you and your tree,
> Were to be killed by men with chainsaws!

Who has the glee now?

**Maisie Grover (10)**
**Mountnessing Primary School, Mountnessing**

## War

War, war is so poor, if you go there in the night
You'll have such a big, big fright.

Grenades, guns, in the air, they are flying everywhere.
Hitler, Hitler, with his bat, don't go near that nasty rat.

Hurt, sick people everywhere,
They'll be winched up in the air.

But always remember war does not compare.

**Alex Horsnell (10)**
**Mountnessing Primary School, Mountnessing**

## Save The World!

Pollution is poisoning the world
It makes it a dirty place.

Stop the war
Live in peace.

Pick the litter up
Put it into a bin.

Don't kill the animals
They will be extinct.

**Harry Strickland (11)**
**Mountnessing Primary School, Mountnessing**

## Stop The Litterbugs

Litter! Litter! everywhere
All these litterbugs they don't care
Litter here! Litter there!
Litter! Litter! everywhere!

Get that rubbish of the street,
Make it look nice and neat,
Animals get their heads stuck in tins,
Put your rubbish in the bins.

Junk on the beaches,
Going in the sea,
Killing all the animals,
Don't you see,
Litter here! Litter there!
Litter! Litter! everywhere!

**Aimee Parker (10)**
**Mountnessing Primary School, Mountnessing**

## Animal Care

Beaches filled with rubbish
Turtles caught in plastic bags
Countryside covered in litter
Hedgehogs stuck in old Coke cans
Am I the only one who cares
About the innocent creatures?
Don't throw your rubbish away
Recycle your cans and reuse your bags
Take your rubbish home with you
And you can care about the animals too.

**Bethanie Monk (11)**
**Mountnessing Primary School, Mountnessing**

## Recycle

This world used to be a wonderful place
To taste and see.
Recycle, recycle, go to the bicycle.
Mother Nature is sad,
Especially when the world is bad.
Be active and don't use plastic,
Be the one to save the planet
And not so much panic.

**Natalie Roy (8)**
**St Peter's Catholic Primary School, Gloucester**

## Every Little Thing Is Going To Be Alright

Every little thing is going to be alright,
So hold on tight,
For a ride in the light.

So this is what we're going to do,
We're going to pick up litter,
And we are going to recycle too.

Don't worry if you see the government,
Tell them to stop litter,
But if they don't, tell them they're bitter,
If you see the Prime Minister, give him a salute,
Then tell him, 'You've got a nice suit.'
Tell him the problem.

This is the end of my poem
Now see if it works for yourself.

**Niamh Valentine (9)**
**St Peter's Catholic Primary School, Gloucester**

## Don't Make Our World Feel In Pain

Don't make our world feel in pain,
Otherwise we'll have to take the blame,
So if we act now,
I'm sure for certain.
We want to see pollution in your policies,
So if we leave Mother Nature in pain,
We're gonna have to do some serious explaining.

So if our parents think it's rubbish,
Think nothing of it,
'Cause when they're worried,
They'll act quick before it makes us sick.

**Katia D'Amato (9)**
**St Peter's Catholic Primary School, Gloucester**

## Stop!

Stop pollution,
Stop the madness,
Stop the Earth from feeling sadness.

God is mad,
God is sad,
Stop the Earth from dying fast.

Stop the shouting,
Stop it now,
Stop the happiness from dying out.

**Tristan Chong (9)**
St Peter's Catholic Primary School, Gloucester

## Take Action

*Honk, honk* cars go by,
Putting smoke up into the sky,
*Crash, bang* on the floor,
Goes the litter on the lawn,
*Plod, plod* goes the paper
Into the bin and down the tip,
Why didn't you recycle it?
*Chop, chop* goes that tree,
Now it floods in the town,
Global warming and other things,
Why don't you take action?
Make a difference, see what you can do.

**Isaura Barr (9)**
**St Peter's Catholic Primary School, Gloucester**

## Do Not Litter!

Do not litter,
It makes me feel bitter,
It makes me sick,
Because it's mostly stuck on sticks,
It's not very keen
Because people get mean,
The Earth's in danger,
So let's be rangers,
Sort it out once and for all,
Before it drive us up the wall.

**Kieran Fox (9)**
**St Peter's Catholic Primary School, Gloucester**

## Our Trashed World

Our world used to be really clean,
Now it's all dirty and mean.
The people who drop litter think they're the boss.
It makes me feel really cross.

Our world is getting thrown around,
All of the junk is on the ground.
Next time throw it in the bin,
And try and recycle all the tin.

There are people in the rainforest making pollution.
Please help them stop, that's a solution.
So is that a very useful tip?
Go back home and listen to it!

**Kimberley Travell (9)**
**St Peter's Catholic Primary School, Gloucester**

# How To Help The Planet!

Always recycle,
Recycle some tins,
Never throw junk,
Except in the bins.

Recycle paper,
Help the place,
Help the world,
Never throw junk in space.

Recycle cardboard,
We can stop this pollution,
Help Mother Earth,
To find a solution.

**Kenneth De La Cruz (9)**
**St Peter's Catholic Primary School, Gloucester**

## Our World

If our world was extinct,
Then all human beings would not exist,
If you see litter,
Don't be a bit bitter,
Go and pick it up
And put it in the bin,
Or I'll be at your door
And I will tell you once and for all,
That our world is dying.
The birds will stop flying,
And all human beings will die.

I feel sad
And it makes me very mad,
That people don't care,
So let's start to share
The wonderful world we live in.

**Zoe Limbrick (9)**
**St Peter's Catholic Primary School, Gloucester**

## Our Earth

Our Earth is like a big balloon,
It's delicate, so please act soon.

I feel so angry when I see people litter,
It makes me feel so sad and bitter.

So please try and stop it,
It's our Earth so don't destroy it.

Mother Earth will be so glad
If we don't make her Earth so bad!

**Mariya Rajesh (8)**
**St Peter's Catholic Primary School, Gloucester**

# Our World

Our world is not a clean place,
But we can make that change.
If we stop littering, it will make a difference.

Our world is getting dirty.
Our world is turning into a rubbish dump.
Our world is messy.

If we don't do something quick,
Our world will just explode.
So if we don't stop being messy,
Our world will be a sad place.

**Jacob Foster (8)**
St Peter's Catholic Primary School, Gloucester

## What's Happening?

Man in the rainforest chopping down trees,
Destroying homes of the monkeys,
You're dropping litter,
Are you feeling bitter?
Don't pollute,
Give the happy world a good salute,
Our future is in our hands,
So please don't destroy our lands,
It makes me sick,
The world looks like a litter pit,
Recycle, recycle,
It is vital.

**Alisha Perkins (9)**
**St Peter's Catholic Primary School, Gloucester**

# The Litter Poem

All the litter makes me sick
If you see some, please act quick.

Recycle tissue
And make it a serious issue.

**Matthew Cantillion (9)**
**St Peter's Catholic Primary School, Gloucester**

# Earth

Earth is our home,
Please don't destroy it,
We cannot make a clone,
So stop the bad habit.

Do not pollute the Earth,
So walk to school,
It can't have another birth,
So win this duel.

Stop the flooding,
It ruins the Earth,
I am annoyed,
Because our Earth's destroyed.

**Shaun Kent (9)**
**St Peter's Catholic Primary School, Gloucester**

## Pollution

Pollution is terrible.
Pollution is bad.
It will only help to make our world sad.

We've all got to help,
And do our best,
To make it better,
In the north, east, south and west.

Pollution is mad.
Pollution is sad.
It doesn't make anyone glad,

    *So stop now!*

**Callum Jake McFarlane (9)**
**St Peter's Catholic Primary School, Gloucester**

## Save Our World

Recycle paper, recycle plastic,
Don't put it in the bin,
Recycle, so remember, recycle,
It all helps for our world.

Put the litter in the waste bin,
Don't put it on the side of the road,
Put it in the waste bin,
It all helps for our world.

Don't cut down the trees,
It makes me sad, it really makes me mad,
If you cut out the trees, the animals can't live.
It all helps the world.

**Been Jude (9)**
**St Peter's Catholic Primary School, Gloucester**

## Grown-Ups Don't Listen!

If grown-ups don't listen,
Maybe kids will,
To stop the pollution,
If we try, we will.

If grown-ups don't listen,
The ice shelf will melt,
The rainforest will die,
Maybe we can help.

If grown-ups don't listen,
We can recycle,
Don't let it waste,
Can we make it good?

If grown-ups don't listen,
We can make a difference.
We made a promise to God,
Let's keep that promise, or else!

**Patrick Sharpe (9)**
**St Peter's Catholic Primary School, Gloucester**

## Save Our World!

Our world is changing,
We have to act soon,
Otherwise it'll burst
Like a big balloon.

Recycle paper,
Recycle bags,
It'll all help
To make our world glad.

Pollution is terrible,
Pollution is bad,
It'll only help
To make our world sad.

I'm begging you please,
Don't drop litter,
It will only make
Our lives bitter.

Please listen,
Take my word,
I'm begging you
To save our world!

**Leo Gregory Ashby (9)**
**St Peter's Catholic Primary School, Gloucester**

## Our World

Our world is a trust,
As we have to make it spotless,
Oh yes, please make it clean.

Our world is a trust,
As we've got to recycle paper,
Oh yes, please make it clean.

Our world is a trust,
As we've got to stop cutting down trees,
Oh yes, please make it clean.

**Allen Shaji (9)**
**St Peter's Catholic Primary School, Gloucester**

# The Big Clean World

The big clean world
Is the best world,
Don't throw litter into space.

The big clean world
Is the biggest world,
Don't throw rubbish in the way.

The big clean world,
Is the cleanest world,
Don't throw litter in the road.

**Shaun Elias (9)**
**St Peter's Catholic Primary School, Gloucester**

## Save Us!

Trees are being cut down everywhere,
And nobody really seems to care.
It makes me crazy, it makes me sad,
It makes me absolutely *mad!*

People are demolishing our great land,
And burying rubbish under the golden sand.
Our world is big, so please keep it clean,
Or even make a recycling machine.

So now I am going to say once and for all,
*Save us, save us, save us all!*

**Baylee Yani Myatt (9)**
**St Peter's Catholic Primary School, Gloucester**

## Our World

Our environment was a lovely place but look what it is now!
No one does anything to help our world, not even a bit,
People just run around going crazy,
And I am staring at them as if to say, 'You're lazy!'

So I shouted out because I was so angry,
'We've got to recycle, so let's go!'

That's the end of my poem,
I hope you learnt something from it.
So let's just help a little bit.

**Sophie Harris (8)**
**St Peter's Catholic Primary School, Gloucester**

## The World One Day

Come on everyone, listen to me,
Come on and listen and you will see
Your house flooded,
Your backyard destroyed,
Everyone knows this is the world one day.

Come on everybody, listen to me say,
Come on everyone, help me save the day.
Global warming, pollution and loads of trash,
If you help me we will clean up in a *flash!*

**Declan McGauley (8)**
**St Peter's Catholic Primary School, Gloucester**

# Walk Don't Drive!

This world used to be a wonderful place,
But now I can see a frown on my face.

Mother Nature is very cross,
Especially when it is very hot.

Cars are useless and they will hurt you one day,
So hurt them first and live your life away!

You're perfectly capable of walking to the shop,
Go walk instead, it's a lot more healthy,
You'll be surprised by the shock!

**Willow Burden (9)**
**St Peter's Catholic Primary School, Gloucester**

## Save The Earth Today

Come all you people, listen to this,
I'm gonna tell you about a crisis.

Think of the Earth as a big, big ball,
If you burst it, we all will fall.

Go on people, help Mother Nature,
You know what, that would just be the best.

The Earth ball is sinking down,
All this is giving me a frown.

We've all gotta save the ozone layer,
Tell it to everyone even the mayor.

All of us have got something to say,
*We're all gonna save the Earth today!*

**Marcus Taylor (9)**
**St Peter's Catholic Primary School, Gloucester**

## Polluted World

Pollution is a really big issue
So recycle our spare tissue.
Our world is a very bad place,
So stop this very big craze.
We can save the environment for everyone to go, *'Wow!'*
Recycle our tin, don't let it go in the bin.
Take pride in our world,
So say a word to save the birds.
Reuse, reduce, recycle,
Follow my rule and give it to your friends.
Our animals are in danger,
So be a ranger.

**Amitha Susan Alex (9)**
**St Peter's Catholic Primary School, Gloucester**

## The Environment

The environment is dying, come and save the day
Before Mother Earth implodes with toxic waste.
My temper is gaining,
Let's stop it now,
Everyone's in danger,
We want it to live, now that's a fact.

Come on everybody, let's save the world.
Thank you for listening,
Hope you make a change.

That's the end of the poem, goodbye!

**Joseph Hill (8)**
St Peter's Catholic Primary School, Gloucester

# World Poem

This is a poem about the world
Recycle things as you do,
Same with tissue,
Plastic bags do not disintegrate
Like other things do.
The very sad part is the world is a mess,
God gave us this world gracefully,
But it is now a kingdom of rubbish.

**Harley Brown Pollok (9)**
**St Peter's Catholic Primary School, Gloucester**

## Pollution Problem

Pollution is a problem,
Think how you and I can work together
To stop this pollution.
*It's a crime!*
Stop this crime, at this time!

Pollution problem, it will never end without you.
There is something wrong with this Earth.
Can you help? You'd be a hero.
With your help, you and I will stop
*Pollution!*

**Lauren McMahon (9)**
**St Peter's Catholic Primary School, Gloucester**

## The Litter Song

Don't throw litter
It's not like glitter
Let's stop it from the flow
Let's get out of our seats
And stop the litter beat
And never let it flow
Or otherwise we will go.
Mayors come along and stop the litter song
We will put it in the bin
And that's the only thing.
Come everyone along
And stop that litter song!

**Tara McGurk (9)**
**St Peter's Catholic Primary School, Gloucester**

# Litter

Litter, litter
It's ever so bitter
'Oh why? Oh why?'
I ask the sky
Why should we care?
It's really not fair
Oh my, oh me
It's a catastrophe
I feel so disgraced
With our human race
What have we done?
It's really not fun.
The world is a disgrace
I can't believe this place!

**Alex Regan (8)**
**St Thomas More Catholic Primary School, Cheltenham**

## Recycle

Imagine if the world was a dump
It puts me in a right grump
I wish the world was a better place
But it's not, it's a disgrace
I love to recycle, it makes me so glad
But when others don't, it makes me mad
We all need to chip in
Otherwise the world will be a rubbish bin.

**Josh Domm (8)**
**St Thomas More Catholic Primary School, Cheltenham**

# Recycling

R ecycling is good for our planet
E veryone can save the world
C an't people put cans in the recycling centre?
Y ou recycle your litter
C an't everyone recycle litter?
L itter goes in the bin
I n the bin there is litter
N ever throw litter on the floor
G o to the recycling centre.

**Leanne Maria Lusmore (8)**
**St Thomas More Catholic Primary School, Cheltenham**

# Rainforest

R ain is very wet
A nts are so very small
I like rainforests
N ew plants grow very quickly
F rogs are everywhere
O pen flowers grow
R ain is see-through
E ggs are hatching noisily
S nakes are slimy
T rees are tall.

**Zea Melania Cuciurean (8)**
**St Thomas More Catholic Primary School, Cheltenham**

## Our Vandalised World

Please! Please! Start to care
About this world that we all share
Why do we destroy the trees
With all the things that live and breathe?
Do not litter on the floor
Littering is against the law
Make this world a better place
Help us save the human race.

**Ben Edwards (9)**
**St Thomas More Catholic Primary School, Kidlington**

## Animals And Extinction

Pandas, butterflies
White lions, dragonflies
Tigers and rhinos
Lobsters and elephants
Why are these animals becoming extinct?

Dodo, mammoth
Sabre-tooth, dinosaur
Forest turtle, blind snake
Oil beetle, rock rat
These were our animals that we used to love

We all need to try to save our world
We all love animals so stop killing them
The world is a better place with our animals
So love all animals like you do your pets.

**Eleanor O'Malley (10)**
**St Thomas More Catholic Primary School, Kidlington**

## Litter, Litter Everywhere

Litter, litter everywhere
Horrible smells in the air
Then stop all litterbugging
Says the government who is nagging
Of all our rubbish on the ground
If we don't we will certainly have found
We would wade through paper, rubbish and mess
And pick up diseases, I would guess
Litter, litter everywhere,

Litter, litter everywhere,
Do people really care?
If the world around us promises
Perhaps the people will recycle and take notice
We could close the landfills and clean the air
If littering we stop and really care
Litter, litter everywhere.

Litter, litter everywhere
So put the rubbish in the bin
Don't throw it around as it would be a sin
We would protect the animals, plants and houses
And clean up the beaches, paths and spaces
We would become wiser and green
And help our environment to be clean!

Litter, litter nowhere!

**Daniel Murray (9)**
St Thomas More Catholic Primary School, Kidlington

# A Heart For The Homeless

'Want a house?'
They always say,
'Can't afford it anyway.'

I'm really weak,
I've got a cold,
People think
I'm fifty years old!

Being beaten up,
I've got rag clothes,
I'm depressed,
With real skinny bones.

I think I'm dying,
I have no food,
People walking by
Are really rude.

Sleeping in darkness,
Creepy witch,
Deathly smell,
Black cold ditch.

Someone's been kind,
They've given me money,
I have a home
And a buddy.

So if you give to others,
You will feel good,
I hope my story's told you
Why you should.

**Lonpe Adeniran (10)**
**St Thomas More Catholic Primary School, Kidlington**

## Need The Rainforests

Save the rainforests, one and all,
Doesn't matter if big or small,
Plant more trees, strong and tall,
We want our wildlife, beautiful or not,
We need the rainforests!
So save the rainforests!

We need the trees,
We need the wildlife,
The animals are beautiful,
And the plants are glorious
We're ruining their homes!
We need the rainforests!
So save the rainforests!

If we knew how much wildlife we hurt,
We'd have to stop,
So start by putting seeds in pots!
We waste lots and lots of trees
Which make paper
And when we waste it all,
Our lovely planet will be dull!
We need the rainforests!
So save the rainforests!

**Megan Keates (10)**
**St Thomas More Catholic Primary School, Kidlington**

# Recycling

Twigs and hay,
Recycle I say,
Plants and grass,
Quick, recycle fast.

Brown, black,
Green and blue,
I can get these
Just for you.

Twigs and hay,
Recycle I say,
Plants and grass,
Quick, recycle fast.

You'll kill the world,
The rubbish will swirl,
The environment will be ruined,
I am frightened of the future.

Twigs and hay,
Recycle I say,
Plants and grass,
Quick, recycle fast.

Spick and span,
I know you can do it,
I know you can.

**Rachel O'Mahoney (10)**
**St Thomas More Catholic Primary School, Kidlington**

## Energy Savers

Energy savers
Do the right thing
Not leaving things
Plugged in.

Switch off lights
When you're not in
TVs and computers
Do the same thing.

Get some solar panels
Convert some energy
And be a good
*Energy saver!*

**Samuel Hazell (9)**
**St Thomas More Catholic Primary School, Kidlington**

## Help People

Help the people who are poor,
Help the people who are homeless,
Help the people who don't have money,
And help the people who are in coldness.

Help the people who are sick,
Help the people who are hungry,
Help the people who sleep on streets,
And help the people who are lonely.

If you can help these types of people,
Then you are a really great person,
And God will forever love you,
Because you helped a fellow human.

**Kiana Bamdad (10)**
**St Thomas More Catholic Primary School, Kidlington**

## Litter

Litter, litter it makes me bitter
When I see it on the ground
Litter, litter it makes me sicker
If I see it in a mound.

Litter, litter cut it down
Before the world turns mouldy brown
Litter, litter reduce it now
Bin it, recycle it, that is how.

Litter's gone, the world is clean
At least it is, in my dream
We love our world all so well
Let's keep it clean, we don't want it to smell!

**Oliver Clark (9)**
**St Thomas More Catholic Primary School, Kidlington**

## Common Factor

We needed to save the animals,
That we can no longer see.
The species and types are many,
None of them mean anything to me.

The pink-headed duck,
Had a run of luck,
The Mascarene coot,
Had been given the boot.

The poor laughing owl,
Had fallen foul,
And whatever happened to the infamous dodo?
I do not know.

There is one common factor,
Man, he could not see,
What he had done to all these creatures,
Which should have meant so much to you and me!

**Katie Smith (9)**
**St Thomas More Catholic Primary School, Kidlington**

## Nature's Kiss

The story of the dodo begins far and wide
On the island of Mauritius where the dodos lived and died.
Before the sailors came, Mauritius was a happy place
Dodos fed on Calvaria trees, full of the sweet embrace

When the ship drifted through the mist, dodos welcomed them
                                                    with opened wings.
But this wasn't such a good idea - the sailors beat them
                                                    with mighty swings.
The only things the sailors wanted were the feathers and the food.
They didn't care about the bird itself, just what it could do for them . . .

So, for being friendly, for being nice
The dodos served an unfair price
One minute a happy life
Then under the pain of the knife.

Killing, killing, all around
This is bad for nature's ground!
If we put a stop to this
We could have the nature's kiss!

Animals!

**Olivia Pickford (9)**
**St Thomas More Catholic Primary School, Kidlington**

# Rubbish Day

Let me tell you a few rules:

What you put in the brown bin
Is garden waste
Pets' leftovers, old rotten leaves
Nothing misplaced.

What you put in the green bin
Are non-recyclable things
Plastic and cardboard
Throw them in - *ding!*
Now *start* recycling!

What you put in the blue bin
Are everyday objects
Paper and cans
Binman collects.

What you put in the composter
Are fruit and veg peelings
Banana skins and carrot peelings
That's what's its filling.

We need you to protect the Earth
Help the environment and yourself
Recycle from the start of your birth
*'Stop the landfills!'* we all shout!

**Bethany Cattell (10)**
**St Thomas More Catholic Primary School, Kidlington**

## Rainforest Ravage

Tree snails, sloths,
Orang-utans, apes,
Spider monkeys, ants,
Trying to escape.

Animals are valuable,
So stop cutting down trees,
Branches waving up to the sky,
Full of green, green leaves.

*Drip, drip,* hear the rain,
*Zzzzz,* insects scuttling,
*Trump, trump,* of the elephant herd.

Please give them your respect,
*Thump, thump,* fall trees,
The forest on fire, blazing.
Please help the environment,
Stop murdering trees!

**Jessica Featherstone (10)**
St Thomas More Catholic Primary School, Kidlington

# It Isn't That Hard

Electricity, pollution and water
We are thinking of the future
We want to make less greenhouse gases
To protect the Earth for our future masses.

Recycle your paper
Recycle your card
Come on now
It isn't that hard!

Planting flowers, bulbs and trees
Is great news for bugs, birds and bees
They can make their homes around our school
Which we all think is really cool!

Recycle your paper
Recycle your card
Come on now
It isn't that hard!

Learning all about pollution
We're all striving to find a permanent solution
Walk instead of using cars
It'll help reduce the world's environmental scars.

Recycle your paper
Recycle your card
Come on now
It isn't that hard!

Let's make some changes in our school
You eco-kids are really cool
We'll work together as a team
A greener planet is our dream.

Recycle your paper
Recycle your card
Come on now
It isn't that hard!

**Eco-School Reps (8-12 yrs)**
**Thomas A Becket Middle School, Worthing**

## Don't Burst The Bubble

The Earth needs our help
Get into action
Help stop global warming.
The Earth needs our help

The Earth needs our help
Don't burst the bubble
Please don't drop litter
Help animals!

The Earth needs our help!

**Natalya Fisher (8)**
**Vale First & Middle School, Worthing**

## How Not To Stop Global Warming

It is colder now than when Jesus was born,
So get out your aerosols because I want it warm.

Cut down the trees, 'cause we don't want to freeze.

Make lots of smoke, so the atmosphere chokes.

To no one's surprise, the sea levels rise.

The rivers flood, the winds get stronger,
I can't see the world lasting much longer.

The government says, 'Global warming's a fact,'
I think it's just a way to get more tax.'

The Romans grew grapes, all along by Goring,
I think global warming is really quite boring.

We've wrecked the world, the damage is done,
So we might as well enjoy the sun!

**Jessica Jackman (10)**
**Vale First & Middle School, Worthing**

# Save The World

The trees, the trees are being cut down,
Save the world, save the golden crown.
When you see litter on the ground,
Pick it up and do it proud.
The ozone layer is about to split,
Take the responsibility to join the sponsorship.
Save the world!

                        Save the world
                        Save the world
                        Do *something now!*

**Lucy Piper (10)**
**Vale First & Middle School, Worthing**

## Global Warming

Beware
Turn off your Wii
Environment needs care
Turn lights off when you leave home
Don't use your mobile phone.

**Emma Duncan (8)**
**Vale First & Middle School, Worthing**

# Help The World

Help us
With the rubbish
And put it in the bin
Everybody pick up rubbish
Recycle all the tins

People help recycle
Recycle all you can
You better start recycling
Help the environment now!

**Ben Colburn (8)**
**Vale First & Middle School, Worthing**

## Save The World! - Cinquain

Reuse
Help our planet
Walk to school every day
Leave the dirty car at your home
You're safe.

**Matthew Votta (7)**
**Vale First & Middle School, Worthing**

## Global Warming

'Why is the ice melting Mummy?'
Said the baby polar bear.
'Because of global warming, darling.'

Global warming is bad
Animals are sad
We need to recycle now.

'What can we do Mummy?'
'Nothing but hope!'

**Georgia Smith (8)**
**Vale First & Middle School, Worthing**

## Endangered Animals

In the rainforest,
there are endangered tigers.
If you want to help,
stop cutting down the trees.

**Amy Little (8)**
**Vale First & Middle School, Worthing**

## Global Warming - Cinquain

Warming
No more battles
Penguins will lose their home
Walk to school, not in cars, cycle
Reuse.

**Max Tozer (8)**
**Vale First & Middle School, Worthing**

## Recycle

R escue the world.
E nvironment is in danger!
C lear up your mess!
Y ou can help by recycling.
C are for animals.
L itter, clean it up!
E lectricity, turn off when leaving the house!

**Jamie Ward (8)**
**Vale First & Middle School, Worthing**

## Save The Environment - Cinquain

Planet
Global warming
Recycle and reuse
There are endangered animals
Action!

**Meredith Furlong (8)**
**Vale First & Middle School, Worthing**

## Reuse

R ecycle paper that you have not used
E co-friendly is a good thing to be
U se the bin
S ave the penguins
E ndangered animals need help.

**Fay Mugridge (8)**
**Vale First & Middle School, Worthing**

# Pollution

P lease do not pollute our world,
O bey the rules of litter,
L ove your world,
L ook after our Earth.
U ndertake to do more recycling.
T ime is running out.
I t is down to you.
O nly if we all help,
N ature can be saved!

**Chloe Honess (10)**
**Vale First & Middle School, Worthing**

## Save The World

Pick up the rubbish
And put it in the bin
Help us save global warming
Act now.

Pick up the rubbish
And put it in the bin
Help save the world
Act right now!

**Lauren McIlrath (7)**
**Vale First & Middle School, Worthing**

## Recycle Now - Cinquain

Our world
Recycle now
Recycle everything
Pick up litter have a shower
Keep clean.

**Jack Cannon (8)**
**Vale First & Middle School, Worthing**

## The Golden Rule

Walk to school, it's the golden rule,
It's cool, cool to walk to school,
You need no fuel to walk to school,
You can even bounce your ball on the way to school,
Walk to school, walk to school,
Why don't you make it your golden rule?

**Hannah Potiphar (9)**
**Vale First & Middle School, Worthing**

## Stop Polluting

P eople messing up the world,
O il from ships kills the birds.
L itterbugs make our streets ugly,
L ess graffiti would be good.
U sing petrol spoils the air,
T oo much smoke and I stop breathing.
I want to save the trees and woods,
O ur animals need our help too.
N ow's the time. It's not too late!

**Bethany Moxham (9)**
**Vale First & Middle School, Worthing**

## Sounds Of Tomorrow

Look at the sky
Look at the ground
I can hear a little sound
Is it a chainsaw
Chopping down a tree?
Is it a choking bumblebee?
For yesterday I could hear a sound
The little bee buzzing round
The chainsaw was far, not near
For I know things are changing
I can hear!

**Lara Miles (9)**
Vale First & Middle School, Worthing

# Recycle

R ecycling is really cool
E verybody does it right
C hildren at home and school
Y ou can recycle day and night
C ardboard, paper, bottles and cans
L ove the world you live in
E nvironment aware, it's in your hands!

**Minni Whiffen (8)**
**Vale First & Middle School, Worthing**

## Litter

L itter is rubbish
I t is bad
T o help the world
T o help God
E veryone pick up litter
R ight, now put it in the bin.

**Brae Parker (8)**
**Vale First & Middle School, Worthing**

## Save

S eals and polar bears are dying
A nimals of the Arctic are in danger
V ow to help save the world
E verybody can make a difference.

    Save electricity.
    Save gas.
    Save water.
    Save the planet!

**Carrie Dollner (9)**
**Vale First & Middle School, Worthing**

# Help The Environment - Cinquain

Go green
Turn off the lights
Save electricity
Help stop global warming today
Help us!

**Katherine Scott (9)**
**Vale First & Middle School, Worthing**

# Bags, Bottles, Newspapers Too

Bags, bottles, newspapers too
All are recyclable, so please help,
That means you!
Helping in small ways
All makes a difference
So your help is needed every day!

**Lauryn Cook (8)**
**Vale First & Middle School, Worthing**

## Global Warming

Please save energy
Recycling's good too
It's good for global warming
And it's a fun thing to do.

**Jodie Ward (9)**
**Vale First & Middle School, Worthing**

# Save Our Home

Earth is our home
And a lovely one she is
So let's help save her now!
Remember, recycle and reuse
Don't waste fuels
Earth needs to be saved
Saved by us all.

**Francesca Collier (8)**
**Vale First & Middle School, Worthing**

## Pollution Solution

Less cars, more bikes,
Children playing with their kites.

Put your rubbish in the recycle bin,
Then we might begin to win.

Remember there is always a solution,
Especially to pollution.

**Harvey Newman (9)**
**Vale First & Middle School, Worthing**

## Why Chop It Down?

Rainforest, rainforest
Why chop it down?
The animals are dying!
Why chop it down?
We need trees for oxygen
Why chop it down?
It looks so beautiful
Why chop it down?
We are destroying the rainforest!
Why chop it down?

**Lois Bevan (10)**
**Vale First & Middle School, Worthing**

## Spring Tree

On the edge of the playground
Dainty blossom decorates a bold spring tree
As the pretty confetti drifts down to the ground
A sudden gust of wind blows it all over me

Small patches of bright blue can be seen
Through the many twigs and leaves
As I look up at the beautiful bold spring tree

As I lie on the ground
And watch my bright spring tree
I am brought back to Earth as my friend yells,
'Come and play with me.'

**Caroline Birch (10)**
**Vale First & Middle School, Worthing**

## Young Writers Information

We hope you have enjoyed reading this book - and that you will continue to enjoy it in the coming years.

If you like reading and writing poetry drop us a line, or give us a call, and we'll send you a free information pack.

Alternatively if you would like to order further copies of this book or any of our other titles, then please give us a call or log onto our website at
www.youngwriters.co.uk

**Young Writers Information
Remus House
Coltsfoot Drive
Peterborough
PE2 9JX**

**(01733) 890066**